NOTE TO SELF

The Authentic Me

My Journey Journal of Validation

By Treca Yvette DeShields, MSW

Cover Art by Patro Ulmer

Calligraphy by Lucila Beaton, LISW-CP

Note to Self

Published by

Hadassah's Crown Publishing, LLC

634 NE Main St., #1263

Simpsonville, SC 29681

ISBN: 978-1-950894-31-4

Printed in the United States of America

Note to Self

Note to Self

Dedication

This book is dedicated to my mother, Mary Ellen DeShields, and my father, Thomas Glenn, for their unconditional love. To my nana, and my grandmother, the Late Ms. Zenora Babb and Ms. Onnie Carolina Glenn for their strength, encouragement, and dedication to their family and their love for God and His people. To the Save Our Youth Choir, my babies, who are now running the world, you are my first love, forever in my heart and prayers.

Note to Self

Content

BIRTHING PLACE

Note to Self

Note to Self

Introduction

The thought of this book came out of my study of John 4:3-42. This is a very familiar passage in the Bible, the story about the woman at the well. As I allowed the Holy Spirit to guide my studies, I saw a lot in this passage concerning our CORE, behaviors, where we learned to be who we are, such as judgement, avoidance, truth, honesty and our authenticity, to name a few. Let's take a journey through these scriptures. Verse three tells us that Jesus left Judaea and went into Galilee. One text states, "He must needs go through Samaria" (John 4:4 KJV). This is important because it was right here my spirit man leaped. "Needs go through Samaria" (John 4:4 KJV) was what I read when my spirit shouted. **God is intentional!** He had to go through Samaria, through the city, (John 4:5 NIV) "near the plot of ground Jacob gave to his son Joseph." In verse six, we learn that Jacob's well was there, and Jesus, as tired as He was from the journey, sat down by the well. It was about noon. In verse seven, when a Samaritan woman came to draw water, Jesus said to her, "Will you give me a drink?" All Jesus did was ask for a drink. Say to yourself, "He is intentional!" He was intentional enough to have a **divine meeting** with the woman at the well. Intentional enough to have a **date, time and place set for her meeting with the Master. Her encounter with Jesus that day set the course for her life.**

John 4:8 NIV reports, "His disciples had gone into the town to buy food." My God! Look at how He does things. **God will move all distractions, familiarities and traditions to reach you. It was the two of them, alone.** It was at the moment when all Jesus asked for was a drink. It was interesting to me how the woman went from responding to His question about a drink to identifying their differences, traditions and dealings. Jesus responded to her, saying if you only knew who asked for the water, you would ask me for a drink and I would give you living water. The woman went on to discuss with Him what He was not able to do based on what she saw on the outside and her perception of Him.

As the conversation continues, she even asks Him if He thought He was better than the one who created the well. Jesus, in His graceful way, continues to respond to the woman by explaining that anyone who drinks from this water will never thirst again. The woman then begins to open up somewhat and says, "Give me of this water so I will never thirst again. Neither will I have to come back here to draw."

I really believe the woman answered without the expectation of Jesus being able to perform the way He did. It is to say "really? Okay. Give me of this water." My reason for saying this is the account of her saying to Him earlier "you don't have anything to draw water with" was a sign of disbelief that he was not able to do what He said He wanted to do. I further believe the reason Jesus asked her the next question was for her to have a clear understanding of who He was and who was standing in front of her.

Now there is a sudden change in the conversation. I call it the "unpeeling" and "unveiling" of the truth. I often say Jesus was continually trying to bring her up to a spiritual level to hear Him and believe in Him, but she continually wanted to keep things in a surface, carnal, traditional and earthly way. Therefore, what did He do? He flipped the script.

Because this woman was not responding to Him talking to her in a spiritual manner, so He talked to her right where she was and in a place she could understand. It's as if I could hear God say, "Okay, since you do not want to come up to where I am, I am going to meet you right where you are. I am going to meet you right where you talk with your girls. I am going to meet you right where you had your last conversation with your significant other. I am going to meet you right on a level, in which we can hold a conversation and right in a place of exposure." As we would say in the old days, "Because it's me and you."

God proceeds in the conversation with the next question. God asks her to "Go, call thy husband, and come hither." The woman answers and says, "I have no husband." Jesus says unto her, "Thou hast well said, 'I have no husband:' For thou hast had five husbands; and he whom thou now hast is not thy husband: in that saidst thou truly." The woman saith unto him, "Sir, I perceive that thou art a prophet. Our fathers worshipped in this mountain; and ye say, that in Jerusalem is the place where men ought to worship." Jesus saith unto her, "Woman, believe me, the hour cometh, when ye shall neither in this mountain, nor yet Jerusalem, worship the Father. Ye worship ye know not what: we know what we worship: for salvation is of the Jews. But the hour cometh, and now is, when the true worshippers shall worship the Father in spirit and in truth: for the Father seeketh such to worship Him.

God is a Spirit: and they that worship Him must worship Him in spirit and in truth." The scriptures go on to say that God reveals Himself to her. The lady leaves and goes into the town to tell everyone, "Come see a man that told me everything I ever did."

This is such a powerful passage. God had to unveil who she really was in order to get to her truth, the truth. We hide from the truth. Where do we hide? We hide in our mistakes, challenges, hurts, fears, disappointments, rejections, meanness, unforgiveness, betrayal, generational curses, pain, traditions, religion and violations. The very thing we do not address becomes the behaviors we face in our future, the behaviors we carry into leadership, the behaviors we carry into relationships, the behaviors we carry at home, the behaviors we carry on our jobs that eventually show up. God had to go right where the woman at the well lived, the place of challenge, the place of disobedience, the hidden place, the place where no one but He can go to cause her to realize who He is. God will reveal himself in the secret places of our hearts.

It was during this conversation with the woman at the well that He revealed a great scripture. "Now they that worship must worship in spirit and truth." I had to have a talk with God about this. My conversation with God was, "How did you give this word to a woman who was in a life of adultery? In my opinion, she was a sexually promiscuous woman who came to draw water in the heat of the day to avoid the crowd because she knew the life she lived and how people in the city felt about her, the one who was rejected, the one who had no voice in her time, the one who was ashamed of who she was, the one who had probably just left her life of transgression. Lord, how did she get such a powerful word? I thought this would be something you would say to David, the man after your own heart. But to the lowest one of these is who you revealed such a powerful word about worship. God's reply to me was, "It is the one right there that I want, the one who no one feels deserves it, that one, yes that one. The stone that builders rejected."

God continued to reveal to me that people can mimic His spirit. They can imitate, pretend, act like Him in order to entertain or even to ridicule. They have a form of godliness. Then, he reminded me of these scriptures in 2 Timothy 3:5-7 KJV, "Having a form of godliness, but denying the power thereof: from such turn away. 6) For of this sort are they which creep into houses, and leap captive silly women laden with sin, lead away with divers lusts, 7) Ever learning, and never able to come to the knowledge of the truth." God continued to say to me truth, "to thine own self be true." You have to be true to you. When you are true to yourself, then you reveal your vulnerable places. When you reveal your vulnerable places, you address your CORE. When you address your CORE, you are not afraid to see you. When you are not afraid to see you, you can be your authentic self. You have to be true to you. So often we look for validation from everyone else when God is the true validator. Validation is being true to yourself. Validation is the ability to look at you and understand that you may not have it all together. You may be completely out of the will of the Father.

Understand that in your weakness, His strength is made perfect. Your validation is allowing Christ your Creator, the One who knows everything about you, to reveal Himself to you. Christ the soul winner. Through Christ and my being true to myself, my being honest with me, I can validate myself. I am worthy. I am able. I am enough, I can do all things. Today, I celebrate me. Today, I choose self-control.

For the next few weeks, we will explore your CORE to help you validate your future. God is intentional and He has a set time for you.

This book has multiple parts, each described below:

- Daily devotional
- Journaling
- Art therapy through freestyle expression
- Weekly reflection takeaway.

Daily Devotional

Each day for 30 days five days a week, there will be a specific scripture, devotional thought, prayer and an action journal point or reflection to process, to write about daily in the journaling section and an authentic expression page, which you can use to create a free-style drawing or write a note of self-affirmation. The purpose of the devotional is to promote spiritual growth and help you identify any CORE places you need to address. Saturday and Sunday are days of reflection and an opportunity to write down your weekly take away.

Journaling

Journal therapy allows a person to become more aware of their thoughts, feelings and behaviors. Journaling helps a person become aware and gain more insight about their feelings to promote personal change and growth. Promoting personal change and growth helps set the course toward a person working on their spiritual and personal goals. Every time a person hears an intentional message, a layer of them has been exposed but never processed. You may hear a message, start working on prompting change but at some point, get stuck with how to move forward. This book allows you to hear a message and search your inner thoughts for personal freedom. God's Word has the ability to address your rejection, loss, fears, disappointments, negative thoughts, unforgiveness, hurt and any other deep personal needs. God's Word has the ability to bring you hope, direction and change.

Art Therapy

The cover of the book says more than what is seen by the eye. The cover will be used as artwork and a beginning process to help each individual identify CORE emotions tied to their current behaviors. Art therapy is used to help individuals identify ways to explore their self-expression in order to gain more personal insight and awareness. Art allows a person to use creative techniques to express themselves artistically. It is noted that art can also be a way to express nonverbal messages, which guide you into a better understanding of your behaviors, in order to resolve deeper issues. Painting can be used as a coping skill to explore your emotion, improve self-esteem, manage addictions, cope with illnesses or disabilities, improve anxiety or depression, and relieve stress. Painting is an opportunity to help you become aware of your self-expression, which leads to a deeper grasp of yourself and your personality. Artistic creation can be used to help reveal one's thoughts and feelings.

In our class, no artistic talent is needed to complete the artwork. Free-style painting of any kind will allow the participant to succeed. It is expected that the participant will find some associations between the creative choice of artwork and their inner life, helping them explore the place of The Authentic ME. The emerging artwork can be used to stir up and springboard reawakening memories, or to tell a story or reveal messages, thoughts or feelings from the unconscious mind. While you are working, you will become mindful and aware of your artistic process, which will cause you to engage in identifying emotions that will become journaling pieces to write about and process daily. Being mindful of your feelings, thoughts and emotions can lead you to identifying CORE places of unresolved emotions that lead you to successful personal validation and accountability.

Note to Self

Personal Affirmation

I am a ready writer.
Who can tell my story better than me?
I am prepared and willing to explore places within my CORE.

The Authentic Me

Authentic

Real, Genuine, Original, Undisputed Original

My Journey Journal of Validation

Journey

Act of moving from one place to another place
Process of personal change and development

Journal

A book used to write down your feelings or thoughts, giving you
an opportunity to collect and process your inner thoughts,
feelings and behaviors.

Validation

Affirmation, Affirming, Validity, Worthiness, Self-Worth

WHO ARE YOU?

Who are you? This is a question of your identity. So often when we hear this saying, we ask "Who is your family and where are you from?" *Who are you?* is an attachment to your name. It can be good or bad, but your name is associated with what you are known for. *Who are you?* could be what you do in life, your role in your family, relationships and career? *Who are you?* is not only a question that can be asked by others, but it is a question you can ask yourself as well. W*ho are you?* could be everything about you and everything you do not know about you. It is our experiences and culture. Your answer now could be totally different from your answer tomorrow, next week, next month or even next year. *Who are you?* is a question I want you to ponder for the next 10 days.

Start a list. Who are you? Here is an example: I am Treca Yvette DeShields. I am a daughter, good friend, social worker, minister of the Gospel, aunt, only child of my mother, daddy's baby, daddy's girl, educator, graduate of an HBCU (Benedict College), graduate of the University of South Carolina, business owner, sister, niece, strategic-thinker, a business-minded and organized lady, mental health professional, black female, 49-year-old native of Clinton, SC, doctoral degree candidate, singer, god daughter, god mother, assault survivor, empowerment coach, business consultant, supervisor, granddaughter, traveler, intellectual, great dresser, funny and genuine person, intercessor and encourager. **Who Are YOU?**

Day 1

Daily Devotional

<u>*You Are His Image*</u>

Scripture

Genesis 1:26, 27

KJV – 26) And God said, Let us make man in our image, after our likeness: and let them have dominion over the fish of the sea, and over the fowl of the air, and over the cattle, and over all the earth, and over every creeping thing that creepeth upon the earth. 27) So God created man in his own image, in the image of God created he him; male and female created he them.

MSG - 26) God spoke: "Let us make human beings in our image, make them reflect our nature. So, they can be responsible for the fish in the sea, the birds in the air, the cattle, And, yes Earth itself, and every animal that moves on the face of earth." God created them godlike, reflecting God's nature. He created them male and female.

AMP - Then God said, Let Us (Father, Son, Holy Spirit) make man in Our image, according to Our likeness [not physical, but a spiritual personality and moral likeness]; and let them have complete authority over the fish of the sea, the birds of the air, the cattle, and over the entire earth, and over everything that creeps and crawls on the earth." So, God created man in His own image, in the image and likeness of God He created him; male and female He created them.

Devotional Thought

We were created in God's image and likeness. His original intent was to create us to reflect Him. What is God's image? God's image is a visual representation of Him. What is God's likeness? The moral qualities and attributes of God, such as showing kindness, sharing His Word, expressing His love, loving others in word and actions, operating in a pure spirit, walking in forgiveness, obeying His Word, and developing a relationship with Him. What are the things that change our image and likeness? What are the things that make you, you? Why does our image stop expressing the attributes and qualities of God? How do we become distracted? What happens? Life! Our image and likeness are influenced by many factors. Our culture, environment, upbringing, family environment, abilities, disabilities, peers, media, experiences, health, family heredity, gender, nutrition, family influence, geographical influences, hormones, socio-economic status, mental status, intellectual ability, emotional status, and social status are all influences that have a great impact on how we see ourselves. It is amazing how we come right out of the womb learning and adapting to life, which later becomes the behaviors, attributes and qualities of who we are. *Who are you?* is the question I want you to ponder today. Why do you act the way you act, think the way you think or move the way you move? How do others see you? What is your social status? What are your titles? What are your roles? *Who are you?* Be true to you. You are the ready writer of your truth.

Prayer

Dear God, show me, me. Help me see myself through your eyes. I want to reflect Your image and likeness.

Day 1
Journaling

Day 1

Authentic Expression

Day 2

Daily Devotional

You Are Fearfully and Wonderfully Made

Scripture

Psalms 139:14

KJV - I will praise thee; for I am fearfully and wonderfully made: marvelous are thy works; and that my soul knoweth right well.

MSG - I thank you, High God—you're breathtaking! Body and soul, I am marvelously made! I worship in adoration—what a creation!

AMP - I will give thanks and praise to You, for I am fearfully and wonderfully made. Wonderful are Your works, and my soul knows it very well.

Devotional Thought

So often we see ourselves through the eyes of others and their opinions. The way we view ourselves will surely have an impact on how others see us. Wanting to be someone we are not and trying to please everyone are other ways we allow ourselves to be influenced by others. We allow others the opportunity to dictate our lives and tell our story. We base our lives on how they feel about us. Take time today to look in the mirror. Take time to look at you. Think about how you allow others to influence who you are. What do you see? Do you like what you see? Know that God was intentional when He made you. He knew all the details, how He would knit you together and how He would make a perfect design of you. You did not just evolve; God created a blueprint, and He created a unique masterpiece. Being you is so easy. Start today!

Prayer

Lord, help me be me. Show me areas of my life I have allowed others to influence, impact and dictate.

Day 2

Journaling

Day 2
Authentic Expression

Day 3

Daily Devotional

<u>*Who Inspired You?*</u>

Scripture

Proverbs 19:20

KJV – Hear counsel, and receive instruction, that thou mayest be wise in thy latter end.

MSG - Take good counsel and accept corrections---that's the way to live wisely and well.

AMP - Listen to counsel, receive instructions, and accept corrections, That you may be wise in the time to come.

Devotional Thought

There are many reasons someone can inspire you in life. It could be your first teacher, someone not giving up when challenged with problems, someone who helped you out, someone who encouraged you, someone who believed in you, a coach, family member, someone you read about, someone who is passionate about helping others or their acts of kindness, an athlete, a famous actor or a superhero. I was inspired by so many wonderful people God allowed to cross my path. Some are alive but many of them are deceased.

Attending public schools in Clinton, SC, I remember Ms. French at MS Bailey Elementary School, who was that place of protection for me because I did not have my mother around. I remember Mrs. Dillard at Martha Dendy Middle School who encouraged me to do better because she expected more out of me. I remember Coach Gray from

Clinton High School who pushed me because she saw my potential in basketball. I remember Mrs. Gouge also at Clinton High School who saw my leadership skills and encouraged me to become a member of FBLA (Future Business Leaders of America). I remember Dr. Davy at Benedict College in Columbia, SC whose class I failed twice, who took me to Chicago, IL, Atlanta, GA and Texas to represent the school. He once told me, "You have every teacher on this hall wrapped around your finger, but not me because I am not going to allow you to have your way. So, call your mother and whoever else you want to because I refuse to let you do what you want to do." This same lady told me she could see me one day being a minister of a great church. It was the instruction of the wise who inspired me. I did not understand at the time, and I really thought some things were a joke. But today, I see the importance of their counsel, instruction and correction. It is that wisdom I walk in today. Who was there for you? Who encouraged you? Who challenged you? Who inspired you?

Prayer

Lord, thank you for every person you allowed to cross my path.

Day 3
Journaling

Day 3

Authentic Expression

Day 4

Daily Devotional

<u>*Great Cloud of Witnesses*</u>

Scripture

Hebrews 12:1

KJV – Wherefore seeing we also are compassed about with so great a cloud of witnesses, let us lay aside every weight, and the sin which doth so easily beset us, and let us run with patience the race that is set before us.

MSG -- Do you see what this means – all these pioneers who blazed the way, all these veterans cheering us on? It means we'd better get on with it. Strip down, start running—and never quit. No extra spiritual fat, no parasitic sins. Keep your eyes on Jesus, who both began and finished this race we're in.

AMP -- Therefore, since we are surrounded by so great of cloud of witnesses [who by faith have testified to the truth of God's absolute faithfulness], stripping off every unnecessary weight and the sin which so easily and cleverly entangles us, let us run with endurance and active persistence the race that is set before us.

Devotional Thought

Death is a mean monster. When death occurs, it feels like pieces of the puzzle have come apart and there is no glue to hold it together again like it was. I often say it is like waves at the beach. Sometimes the waves will touch the surface of an area and at other times it will overflow the same area. Sometimes, you will feel it a little and at other times it will be overwhelming as if it just occurred. Allow yourself to feel. Feel just how you need to feel. Grieving is a must, and it is okay. Grieving is not forgetting. It allows you to free yourself of the things that are bound to the person lost, such as objects or experiences. I often think about the loved ones I have lost. The memories, the good times and the bad times. The impact they have had on my life. They are still alive; they live on in me. They have become my cloud of witnesses who are cheering me on. Cheer on Lillie Pearl Cunningham, Onnie Carolina Glenn, Zenora Nana Babb, Tina Glenn, Ann Babb, Rome Babb, Jerry Glenn, Phillip Glenn, Uncle Wood, John Rivers, Julia Bailey, Ma Miller, Dorothy Attaway, Daisy Bell Metts, Maggie Craig, Claria Wilson, Soror Mable Wynn, Laura Sturkey, Ms. Bertha Brewster, Floree Garrett, Robert Golden, Carol Higgins, Kenny Glenn, Jr., Little, Margaret Anne Carter, Joyce Franklin, Cindy Turner, Marvin Shumpert, Mike Nelson, JD, ET, Junus Cunningham, Brenda Boyd, Donald Robinson and Gracie Lee to name a few. You are the wind, the push, the encouragement beneath my wings. Who is in your cloud of witnesses? Write about them today. What are your memories? Who are you?

Prayer

Lord, help us to not get overwhelmed with grief but to know you are our help, strength and refuge. In you, we put our trust.

Day 4
Journaling

Day 4

Authentic Expression

Day 5
Daily Devotional
The Tribe

Scripture

Romans 12:5

KJV - So we, being many, are one body in Christ, and everyone members one of another.

MSG – So, since we find ourselves fashioned into all these excellently formed and marvelously functioning parts in Christ's body, let's just go ahead and be what we were made to be, without enviously or pridefully comparing ourselves with each other, or trying to be something we aren't.

AMP - So we, who are many, are [nevertheless just] one body in Christ, and individually [we are] parts one of another [mutually dependent on each other].

Devotional Thought

When I think about my tribe, I think about family. I think about our love, compassion and support for each other. I think about our love for God and sense of unity. I am blessed to have great relationships on both my maternal and paternal sides of my families. Family was instrumental in teaching me about relationships and has a great effect on who I have grown to be. My tribe existed to create a sense of safety, belonging, support, care, goals and guidance in defining purpose in my life. This was the place I learned respect, morals and values. Family is important to me and has been the greatest influence in my life because it taught me how to serve, celebrate and honor one another. Multiple people have played a role in shaping me into the person I am today. The saying "It takes a village to raise a child" is so true. This African proverb speaks volumes to me because it took an entire community of people interacting, providing unconditional love, inspiring, teaching, communicating, guiding, role modeling, being consistent, concerned, patient with an open heart; providing physical, emotional, social and intellectual support, which allowed me to grow in a safe and healthy environment. My tribe and your tribe may be totally different, but some impact has made the difference in your life. Think about it, ponder over it, and reflect on it. Who is your tribe? Is it your family or the community you were raised in? Your church family? Is it linked to your economic, cultural or social status? Is it those you share a common culture with? The purpose of the family and community is to build relationships. What do the relationships in your tribe reflect?

Prayer

Dear God, thank you for family, community and every person you have allowed to be an impact in my life. Thank you for sending the right people in my life during the right season of my life.

Day 5
Journaling

Day 5

Authentic Expression

Weekly Reflection &

Take Away

Day 6

Daily Devotional

I'm Encouraged

Scripture

Hebrews 10:24-25

KJV – And let us consider one another to provoke unto love and to good works: Not forsaking the assembling of ourselves together, as the manner of some is but exhorting one another: and so much the more, as ye see the day approaching.

MSG – Let's see how inventive we can be encouraging love and helping out, not avoiding worshiping together as some do but spurring each other on, especially as we see the big Day approaching.

AMP - And let us consider [thoughtfully] how we may encourage one another to love and to do good deeds, not forsaking our meeting together [as believers for worship and instruction], as is the habit of some, but encouraging one another; and all the more [faithfully] as you see the day [of Christ's return] approaching.

Devotional Thought

Encouragement is key. We all look for someone to encourage us. Encouragement keeps us feeling confident in ourselves and it pushes us to become our best selves. When someone offers us encouragement, it motivates us and shows us that they care. Encouragement lifts us up. I have had a lot of encouragement in my life by so many important people I love. But one day, an encouragement provoked me to change and to do something I have never done before, to write a book. I have been blessed to be the chaplain for the finest: Anderson Alumnae Chapter of Delta Sigma Theta Sorority, Inc. in Anderson, South Carolina for nine years. I was grateful for the appointment by the past chapter presidents, including Soror Lori Brewton, Soror Karen Glenn and Soror Tracy Richardson. It was an honor to provide monthly spiritual inspirational moments for my sorors. I was grateful for the opportunity and I did not take it lightly. I always seek God's guidance for a Word to share at each meeting.

One particular Saturday after a meeting, I was approached by Soror Mable Wynn and asked if she could see my notes on what I shared. I told her I did not have any notes. I only wrote a scripture and allowed God to give me the rest. She replied, "Oh my God! You got that from your head? Oh my, this is some good stuff. You really need to consider writing them down." I asked her, "Do you really think what I share monthly is good?" She responded, "Yes! It is great. I just can't believe you do not have it written down." This conversation encouraged me to start writing my devotionals down and a lot of them are a part of this book. It was Soror Wynn who encouraged me to do more with what God has given me.

I remember going to see her a few days before she passed and sharing that same story with her family. They were so inspired by our relationship that they asked me to do her eulogy. I was thinking me….what? Do you know who Soror Mable Wynn, Clemson professor, community leader, well-known dancer and dance instructor is? Surely you all could find someone else besides me, but again at her death she taught me another lesson. I could hear her say, "Yes, Treca. You. You are the one and we, God and I will help you make this a teachable moment.

At that moment, I pondered what I would say about a woman of great virtue. The lesson or the teachable moment begins with talking about their life and what they taught you while living. Soror Wynn taught others to live life to the fullest regardless. She taught me to have faith and believe, to encourage and lift others. She taught me to keep pressing on, to love in spite of, how to be faithful and committed, how to be prepared and how to invest in my days on earth. She taught me how to bring movement to life when challenges come my way. She was a dancer and she taught me how to dance through my problems, position myself to move when challenges, trials, tribulations come. "Treca, keep moving. Don't stop. Just move. Just dance. Heel, toe, heel, toe slide, slide, slide, slide. When you do not understand and you feel like giving up, position yourself because some movement keeps you moving. Don't stop and dance, Treca. Heel, toe, heel, toe, slide, slide, slide. Keep it moving!"

So, what do I say to you today? Keep it moving! Be encouraged. Live your life daily. Identify ways you can encourage and build someone else up. Encourage someone today. Restore someone's faith. Be positive. Inspire change to better someone's life today. Speak a kind word. Share love. God's love. Soror Mable Wynn (1/8/2020) will forever be in my heart.

Prayer

Dear God, use me today to be a path of light to someone as I travel through this day.

Day 6

Journaling

Day 6

Authentic Expression

Day 7

Daily Devotional

<u>*Mama's Baby, Daddy's Girl*</u>

Scripture

Exodus 20:12

KJV – Honor your father and your mother, that your days may be long in the land that the Lord your God is giving you.

MSG – Honor your father and mother so that you'll live a long time in the land that God, your God, is giving you.

AMP - Honor (respect, obey, care for) your father and your mother, so that your days may be prolonged in the land the Lord your God gives you.

Devotional Thought

My parents. Are my parents perfect? No, but they are perfect for me. Where do I begin? I want to start first by saying "Thank you!" Thank you for being the **BEST PARENTS EVER**. You both have shown great love to me, always supportive, allowing me to be the authentic person I am. Always letting me make the decision, but offering me guidance, advice, support and options. I am independent because of your willingness to trust me to do things for myself and handle things on my own. I am a leader because you gave me good tools for my future. I often say my mother loves me through the eyes of God. She knows what I need, when I need it and what to do at any given time. She is always there no matter what, my biggest supporter and greatest fan. My father is my inspiration, protector, coach, mentor and business partner. We are always tossing thoughts and ideas around. He is the one who will talk about the elephant in the room, the uncomfortable place to provoke me to think about different aspects of a situation. Wow! What a great combination. When I think about my parents, I often think about the lyrics of a song by Billie Holiday. "Them that's got shall get, them that's not shall lose, so the Bible said and it still is news. Mama may have; Papa may have. But God bless the child that's got his own, that's got his own."

This may not be your story. You may have not had the same experience with your parents. Your parents may be deceased. You may not even know your parents. You may have been abused by your parent, but one thing is for sure. You are here because of them. Are your parents perfect? No, but they are perfect for you. Take time today to reflect on your relationship with your parents. Has your relationship with or without your parents affected your social, physical, mental and emotional health? What are some behaviors you exhibit now due to your relationship with your parents? How do you feel about your relationship with your parents? What did you learn from your parents? In what ways are you like your parents? Write down your feelings concerning your parents. Don't be afraid to feel. Feel what you need to feel and say what you need to say.

Prayer

Lord, I thank you for my parents. Continue to show them your love and strengthen them to walk in your will and purpose.

Day 7
Journaling

Day 7

Authentic Expression

Day 8

Daily Devotional

<u>*How Did I Get Here, in This Place?*</u>

Scripture

Psalm 37:23

KJV – The steps of a good man are ordered by the Lord: and he delighteth in his way.

MSG – Stalwart walks in step with God; his path blazed by God, he's happy.

AMP – The steps of a [good and righteous] man are directed and established by the Lord, And He delights in his way [and blesses his path].

Devotional Thought

It started on March 30, 1990. My life was transformed in more ways than one. I suffered a brutal assault during which I was stabbed nine times, a hair's breadth from death because one of the wounds almost severed a main artery in my neck. Prior to the incident that left me physically and emotionally scarred, I was at a spiritual crossroad in my life. It was during this time in my life I contemplated completely surrendering to God, but I did not make a full commitment to Him.

A near-death out-of-body experience on the operating table after I was stabbed left me with an ultimatum from God. I could choose to remain in the afterlife, or I could return and spend my life serving God. I chose God. That's how I got here. It was this moment that I surrendered it all and gave my life to God. During this moment of my life, my family was devastated but very supportive. How this could be was a question often asked. Why did this happen to you? Not you! We all pushed through the long nights and hard days. I pushed through looking at wounds, not knowing how my future would be impacted. My family was there, friends were there. I had everything I needed and wanted.

Years passed and I wonder why I had certain reactions and emotions. Why did I have a numb feeling? Why did I have this uncontrollable rage? Why did I have avoidance of emotions? It wasn't until I began my journey to earn a Master of Social Work that I realized the feelings and behavior were associated with the trauma I experienced. While completing an assignment one night, I began to think about and process my feelings concerning the trauma. I realized I had not dealt with the CORE place. I realized these feelings, emotions and behaviors were being manifested in my leadership, relationships and ministry. How do I deal with this was a question I asked myself? I began to realize that a therapist was not the answer because I have faith and there is no way I was going to talk with anyone else when I have God. These were my thoughts about my situation. I thought if I went to see a therapist, I was allowing someone else's guidance over my life instead of God. So, I struggled with going to see a therapist yet knew something was off.

After struggling for years with the trauma, deaths, crisis, business, life and my faith versus seeing a therapist, I finally made the decision to give therapy a try. I remember being in my favorite doctor's office. Dr. A. Jones said to me that on a scale of one to ten, Treca I have seen you at a four or maybe a five. But now you are a 10 and I need you to consider taking some medication or seeing someone. She reminded me that I needed to go into this in the role of the patient, not the therapist. I laughed because in my mind I was trying to control the situation to fix myself. The therapist needing therapy; the leader needing help. The minister needing counsel. I was thinking, "I will show you." I am a therapist. I work with this every day. I know the interventions to use. I will not break or open up to someone I do not know. I agreed to see someone. Oh well.

I walked in the therapist's office and before I knew it, I was in tears. It was the active listening, the attention given to what I was saying, the prompting of questions and the help of connecting to my spirituality that were all beneficial and important therapeutic accommodations used to help me process some deep, untouched places. Wow! A deep womb opened that can now prepare for healing. I realized then that God can use other professionals to help with your inner healing.

Are there times you remember when God was there for you? Are there places in which you need to search your CORE? Do you need to talk to someone about some deep wombs? Are there things you think about or cope with at least one hour each day? Are there things that cause you embarrassment? Do you often avoid others? Are there things that have negatively affected your work, school or relationships? Are you feeling overwhelmed, fatigued, angry, resentful or enraged? Are you feeling hopeless? If so, seek counsel. It can be spiritual or professional, but get help. It is okay. Sometimes, we need help. Ask God to guide you to the right place so you are able to receive the help you need.

Prayer

Lord, I thank you that there is safety in the multitude of counsel. Thank you for guiding my footsteps to safe places for healing.

Day 8

Journaling

Day 8

Authentic Expression

Day 9

Daily Devotional

<u>*Let's Talk About What Matters - YOU*</u>

Scripture

Ephesians 2:10

KJV – For we are workmanship, created in Christ Jesus unto good works, which God hath before ordained that we should walk in them.

MSG – He created each of us by Christ Jesus to join him in the work he does, the good work he has gotten ready for us to do, work we had better be doing.

AMP – For we are His workmanship [His own master work, a work of art], created in Christ Jesus [reborn from above—spiritually transformed, renewed, ready to be used] for good works, which God prepared [for us] beforehand [taking paths which He set], so that we would walk in them [living the good life which He prearranged and made ready for us].

Devotional Thought

Who are you? We get caught up in the nonsense of the world. We are absorbed with school, career, work, hobbies, families and so many other activities that consume our time. We often feel insignificant, lost and challenged. We get caught up in being so much to everyone else that we forget we matter. Let me remind you, you are not an accident. You matter! You are special, and there are people you are connected to that you have the ability to change their lives. From the beginning of time, God had you in mind. There are no unplanned or unpurposed people. He has a plan for you. You have to look to Him to find your purpose, since He created you. Therefore, it is in Him we will find our meaning, purpose, origin, cause, plan, motivation, intent, significance and destiny. It is when we realize we are God's creation, He made us for His purpose, and He has an amazing plan for our lives that we begin to understand why we matter. As you reflect today, ask yourself these questions. What are the things I have put before God? In what areas of my life do I feel insignificant? How is my life reflecting God's plan? How can I start today living a life of purpose? Repeat these phrases: "I matter." "I will live my life like I matter." Write this statement and reflect on it today. "I matter because…"

Prayer

Lord, thank you for shaping and preparing me to walk in my purpose. Father, I ask that you give me fresh vision daily. Open my eyes, ears, mind and heart to your vision so that I can live my purpose.

Day 9
Journaling

Day 9

Authentic Expression

Day 10
Daily Devotional
<u>*Commit It*</u>

Scripture

Proverbs 16:3

KJV – Commit thy works unto the Lord, and thy thoughts shall be established.

MSG – Put God in charge of your work, then what you've planned will take place.

AMP – Commit your works to the Lord [submit and trust them to Him], And your plans will succeed [if you respond to His will and guidance].

Devotional Thought

Regardless what you have had to deal with in your life, you have to commit it to God. Everything concerning us, including all of our hurts, insecurities, pain, heartache and disappointment have to be committed to him. We have to search our hearts and be true to ourselves. We have to give God all of our concerns, the good, bad and ugly. Why is it that we hold back when he already knows? He is waiting on us to bring it to Him. God promised to give us life and life more abundantly when we leave our old selves behind and follow Him. We have to commit it totally to him withholding nothing, giving it all to Him. He is waiting on us to tell Him what's concerning us so He can help. What is *commitment*? It is a promise to do something or make something happen. It is dedicating ourselves to the cause of being better. God is a great manager of our concerns. It is in Him we will find our peace. When we live under His Lordship, we will find our happiness and success. We have to completely commit and depend on God. When we depend on Him, He will establish, bring about or cause our plans to come to pass. We can expect God to bring our plans into fruition in His way and His time. We have to be willing to do our part.

As we end this week, think about what you need to commit, release or give over to God. Where are the places in your life you rely on your own strength instead of God? Your hurts, insecurities, pain, heartache, disappointments and behaviors come from a CORE place. STOP running after things. STOP avoiding it, whatever it is. Arrest it and address it. Reflect on the CORE places you need to give Him complete and full control.

Prayer

Lord, help me continuously increase my awareness that you are my sustenance. Help me rest in your strength. Help me wholly commit my walk and life to you.

Day 10
Journaling

Day 10
Authentic Expression

Weekly Reflection & Take Away

_____

_____

_____

_____

_____

_____

_____

_____

_____

_____

_____

_____

_____

_____

_____

_____

Note to Self

WHO ARE YOU REALLY?

When no one else is around and it is just you, who are you? What do you see, how do you feel? Are you faced with fears and doubts? Think about it? Are you who everyone else sees on a daily basis or are there things you deal with when you look at you? When you look deeper within your eyes, what do you see? What are you reminded of? Do you see someone who has faced a lot of things in life but is still here to share the story? Do you see someone who has known loss, self-doubt, joy and gratitude? Do you see someone who is good enough? What do you see? When my family looks at me, what do they see? When my friends look at me, what do they see? When a stranger looks at me, what do they see? Do you see flaws or imperfections? Who are you really? **Who Are YOU Really?**

Day 11

Daily Devotional

<u>Who or What Is Holding You Hostage?</u>

Scripture

Ephesians 6:12

KJV – For we wrestle not against flesh and blood, but against principalities, against powers, against the rulers of darkness of this world, against spiritual wickedness in high places.

MSG – And put them to use so you will be able to stand up to everything the Devil throws your way. This is no afternoon athletic contest that we'll walk away from and forget about in a couple of hours. This is for keeps, a life or-death fight to the finish against the Devil and all his angels.

AMP – For our struggle is not against flesh and blood [contending only with physical opponents], but against the rulers, against the powers, against the world forces of this [present] darkness, against the spiritual forces of wickedness in heavenly (supernatural) places.

Devotional Thought

From the beginning of time, Satan has studied human nature, behaviors, thoughts and tendencies. It is his plan to weaken us and the world. He does this by trying to remind us of generational curses, unbelief, shame, pain, death, chronic hopelessness, fears, restless anxiety, mental and physical torment, guilt, lack of knowledge, challenges and anything else he can use to diminish us and God's purpose for our lives. When man fell in the beginning, the enemy immediately used shame and humiliation as a consequence to judge man's fall. Bondages with your authority have the ability to cripple us and keep us from walking in our greatest potential. Bondages can rob us of our destiny. The scripture today reminds us that we do not fight against flesh and blood but powers, forces, darkness, spiritual wickedness in high places. Jesus has the power and authority to cast out and free us of every oppressed and demonic spirit that is holding us hostage. God's Word makes us aware of who we are really fighting. We have to daily speak His Word, His promises concerning our situation. I am grateful we have a Master, Savior, Redeemer Jesus who did not leave us to fight alone or to self-destruct, but in Him we have the victory to overcome the world. Jesus died for the remission of sin. We have to repent, turn completely away from the bondage, give things totally to Him, and He will forgive us, giving us a clean record. What is holding you hostage? Who is holding you hostage? Think about the places you need freedom. There is freedom in Christ. Free yourself of the bondage and move in what God has called you to do.

Prayer

Lord, thank you for allowing me to identify what behaviors, thoughts and tendencies have held me hostage. Free me from the bondage that has been holding me captive from my destiny.

Day 11

Journaling

Day 11
Authentic Expression

Day 12
Daily Devotional
By Any Means Necessary

Scripture

Ephesians 6:16

KJV – Above all, taking the shield of faith, wherewith ye shall be able to quench all the fiery darts of the wicked.

MSG – Be prepared. You're up against far more than you can handle on your own. Take all the help you can get, every weapon God has issued, so that when it's all over except the shouting, you'll still be on your feet.

AMP – Above all, lift up the [protective] shield of faith with which you can extinguish all the flaming arrows of the evil one.

Devotional Thought

There are so many things that can and attempt to keep us from the will of God. The fiery darts of the enemy have been flying since the conception of our life doing their damage trying to find a place or reach a mark on those whose armor is deficient. It is during these times of being unprotected that the wicked one will use principalities to convince you that you are not good enough and that you are not worthy. The enemy will consistently present sin as evidence in order to try to blackmail you into giving up.

When I think about fiery darts, I think about how the enemy tries to ambush our minds with piercing thoughts, a sudden temptation to do wrong, furious suggestions of evil and sudden thoughts that wound, penetrate and torment the soul. There is also the fight we face within with the carnal man, the old man, the flesh. These are the darts that the enemy uses to distract us from what truly matters.

What happens when these darts hit their targets? So often we blame God. God doesn't use evil to temp others, and He cannot be tempted by evil. It is our own desires that trap us and cause us to be dragged off into our own will. It is our desires which make us sin, and when sin is committed, it leaves us dead. What are the darts of your life today? What are the things that the enemy uses to tempt you? You have to continue without any hesitation or doubt. By any means necessary. So often when we hear this phrase it can mean leaving open all available tactics in order to get the desired ends. When I think about this phrase in relationship to God, I think about regardless of what the enemy tried to bring, shoot or throw our way, we have to fight daily to ensure we stay committed to God's will. We have to face it head on, break it down, address the obstacles, stay positive and know that God has provided a way of escape.

Prayer

Lord, I thank you that you have assigned ministering angels to me to pull out every dagger, arrow, spike and flaming dart that the enemy has thrown at me over the years. I cancel every demonic assignment in Jesus' name.

Day 12

Journaling

- -

- -

- -

- -

- -

- -

- -

- -

- -

- -

- -

- -

- -

- -

- -

Day 12

Authentic Expression

Day 13

Daily Devotional

<u>Negativity Has No Place in Your Life</u>

Scripture

Philippians 4:8

KJV – Finally, brethren, whatsoever things are true, whatsoever things are honest, whatsoever things are just, whatsoever things are pure, whatsoever things are of good report; if there be any virtue, and if there be any praise, think on these things.

MSG – Summing it all up, friends, I'd say you'll do best by filling your minds and meditating on things true, noble, reputable, authentic, compelling, gracious-the best, not the worst; the beautiful, not the ugly; things to praise, not things to curse.

AMP – Finally, believers, whatever is true, whatever is honorable and worthy of respect, whatever is right and confirmed by God's Word, whatever is pure and wholesome, whatever is lovely and brings peace, whatever is admirable and of good repute; if there is any excellence, if there is anything worthy of praise, think continually on these things [center your mind on them, and implant them in your heart].

Devotional Thought

There are moments in our lives when we have to deal with negative people. Negative people focus on their own faults or others' faults. They are quick to point out and notice shortcomings with their comments, resulting in someone being or feeling put down, assuming the worst in any situation, approaching things from a pessimistic point of view. They disguise their negativity by using humor or sarcasm. Wasting time addressing negative things isn't justification. It's a sign that you are in bondage, bound by someone else. Negativity can cause chronic anxiety, which leads to chemical and physical changes in the body. When one is faced with chronic anxiety, it is very predictable that it may affect your body functions in a negative way.

Who are the negative people in your life? Identify them and in what way they bring negativity to you. When we have negativity in our lives, Philippians 4:8 reminds us to focus on our ability to rejoice. When we focus on positive things, we are able to experience peace through the power of God. We have to set our attention on positive things. Being able to bring awareness to negativity allows an opportunity for more beauty into our lives, and there will be less room for anxiety.

What are ways we can become aware of negativity around us? Learn to give positive action to your thoughts. Rather than resisting what is undesirable and what you do not want, identify ways to replace these thoughts with what you do want. Focus on good things rather than occupying your minds with the things that life throws and worries. You can accomplish this by focusing on these things: Whatsoever things are true, authentic, real and genuine. Whatsoever things are honest, worthy, excellent and honorable. Whatsoever things are just, upright, righteous and virtuous. Whatsoever things are pure, innocent, modest and clean. Whatsoever things are of good report, think on these things.

Prayer

Lord, help me embrace your tranquility, love and peace so that my mind can be at ease. I break every spirit of negativity now in Jesus' Name. I choose to speak positivity into my life daily. Amen.

Day 13

Journaling

Day 13
Authentic Expression

Day 14

Daily Devotional

<u>Forgiveness</u>

Scripture

Colossian 3:13

KJV – Forbearing one another, and forgiving one another, if any man have a quarrel against any: even as Christ forgave you, so also do ye.

MSG – Forgive as quickly and completely as the Master forgave you.

AMP – Bearing graciously with one another, and willingly forgiving each other if one has a cause for complaint against another; just as the Lord has forgiven you, so should you forgive.

Devotional Thought

Think and write about it today. Have you forgiven everyone in your life you need to forgive? Take time today to really think about that question. Is it your spouse, family member, friend or coworker? There are times when others are asking us for forgiveness. We have to look deep within ourselves. Think about it. Do you have lingering, intense, persistent bitterness in your spirit? Do you constantly blame others? I believe the person we most need forgiveness from is ourselves. When you have unhealthy feelings or emotions about others, who are we hurting the most? These feelings are literally eating a hole in us. Unforgiveness is a weight. It hinders us from flying high. Forgiveness, whether we are giving or receiving, is powerful. When we forgive, it allows us to show love. Love is the greatest thing we can give our family and friends. Forgiveness allows us to heal and be restored.

Start today moving towards forgiveness. Give yourself permission to remember those places of forgiveness, places of violation. Was it your childhood, family, school life, friendship or relationship? Be true about your feelings; talk about your emotions and anger. Take time today to explore your feelings, emotions and anger. Write it down. Ask yourself, who are you angry/bitter with? What do you know about the feeling, emotions or anger you are exploring? How do they impact you? Make the choice to forgive.

You owe it to yourself to start exploring the possibilities of forgiveness and be willing to forgive. Forgiveness is for you. Take the time needed to explore those places. It may bring up old emotions. There may be places where things are still there, deep inside you and you are beginning to bring it to the surface. That's good processing. Know you are worth it. You are worth the time it takes to process those places. So often we have hidden emotions which drive us to live unconsciously repeating and sharing painful experiences over and over. These experiences become our behaviors of today. Forgiveness frees our hearts.

Prayer

Lord, forgive me for those I have done wrong and those who have done wrong to me. Cleanse me daily of the tendency to keep record of wrong-doing, but help me to acknowledge you in all my ways so you can direct my path.

Day 14
Journaling

Day 14

Authentic Expression

Day 15

Daily Devotional

Let It GO!!!

Scripture

1 Peter 5:7

KJV – Casting all your cares upon him; for he careth for you.

MSG – Live carefree before God; he is most careful with you.

AMP – Casting all your cares [all your anxieties, all your worries, and all your concerns once and for all] on Him, for He cares about you [with deepest affections, and watches over you very carefully].

Devotional Thought

When we have been hurt deeply, it is hard to let go of the hurt. As a matter of fact, we hold on pretty tightly. It is our human nature. A lot of times we aren't ready to let go. To be honest, we start to think others deserve to suffer. This only perpetuates the cycle of suffering, causing us to remain a victim. If you find yourself in this place, you are carrying too much stuff. What are you wearing? Are you wasting time addressing negativity? This is not justification; it is a sign you are still in bondage. Is it emotional baggage from unresolved emotional issues, past trauma or stressors? Is it secrets? Understand that secrets can hold you hostage and others captive, unbeknownst to them. These are the things that tend to hold you in bondage in your mind and your physical body. Release yourself of the extra baggage. Let it go. Cast your cares on the Master for He cares for you. Holding on to hurt and unhealthy emotions produces different types of stress chemicals that begin to flood our bodies and make us sick, physically and emotionally. Even when it hurts, we have to be willing to let it go. We have every right to feel that the thing you are dealing with is an unforgiveable act. You may have been physically or sexually abused or a victim of a horrible crime. I am not in a position to downplay and I will not trivialize your situation by suggesting anything will make it right or cause you to forget it. I want you to realize you are not alone and there may be others who have suffered some similar hurts. Self-forgiveness is important when you are working on letting go. Do not give your power over to people. When you do, you are no longer in control of your own life. Chose to have power over your life. Know you have the power to choose.

Today, identify those places of deep hurt. Self-awareness is a step toward healing. It is okay to perceive, know and feel. Self-awareness leads to building your confidence. This may even be a great time to reach out to receive additional support. Letting go can be a hard and hurtful thing, but now that you are aware and mature understand it is a great opportunity for growth and new experiences. Say out loud "I love and have been in love with some things, but I love myself enough to let these things or habits go. I am done with things that hold me hostage." Ask God now to help you identify those places, guide you in the right direction for healing and start writing your plan on how you can begin to move forward to freedom. He will equip you to walk out every aspect of your life. Prepare to be dressed and to be found in Him. He is most careful with you.

Prayer

Lord, help me address the deep places today with no denial. Guide me to the place of safety and healing in you!

Day 15

Journaling

Day 15

Authentic Expression

Weekly Reflection &

Take Away

Day 16

Daily Devotional

That Was Then,

This Is NOW!!

Scripture

Romans 12:1-2

KJV– I beseech you therefore, brethren, by the mercies of God, that ye present your bodies a living sacrifice, holy, acceptable unto God which is your reasonable services. And be not conformed to this world but be ye transformed by the renewing of your mind, that ye may prove what is that good, and acceptable, and perfect, will of God.

MSG– So here's what I want to do, God helping you: Take your everyday ordinary life- your sleeping, eating, going to work, and walking – around life and place it before God as an offering. Embracing what God does for you is the best thing you can do for him. Don't become so well-adjusted to your culture that you fit into it without even thinking. Instead, fit your attention on God. You'll be changed from inside out. Readily recognize what he wants from you, and quickly respond to it. Unlike the culture around you, always dragging you down to its level of immaturity, God brings the best out of you, develop well-formed maturity in you.

AMP– I appeal to you therefore, brethren, and beg of you in view of (all) the mercies of God, to make a decisive dedication of your bodies (presenting all your members and faculties) as a living sacrifice, holy (devoted, consecrated) and well pleasing to God which is your reasonable (rational, intelligent) service and spiritual worship. Do not be conformed to this world (this age), fashioned after and adopted to its external, superficial customs, but be transformed (changed) by the entire renewal of your mind by its new ideals and its new attitude so that you may prove for yourself what is the good and acceptable and perfect will of God, even the things which are good and acceptable and perfect (in His sight for you).

Devotional Thought

SHOUT "No more wasted time!" Today fall out with and away from alcohol, tobacco, drugs, problems, criticism, anger, negative behaviors, low self-esteem, poverty, lack of concern, frustration, jealously, lack and fear. You are no longer in control of your own life. Cast your cares on God. He is the sustainer of your life. Today, choose faith over worry. Today, do not lean on yourself, but acknowledge God and He will direct your path. Today, lay your burdens, hurts, rejections, disappointments and challenges at the feet of Jesus. Think about the things you have worked on the last few days. Continue to release them to God. You have to be committed to start, do and finish what is needed for complete healing in your life. You have to totally surrender everything about your life over to God.

I am reminded of God speaking to me one day about the three "yeses." He said to me that in this walk with Him, we have to give the three "yeses." *Yes* to salvation, *Yes* to the Spirit of God to lead us and *Yes* to be SOLD OUT. We have to give Him everything. How will you face today, the next moment, the next minute or the next opportunity? You have to know Him for yourself. You have to take responsibility for the destiny God has given you. Take 100% responsibility of you. You have to level up. You have to make a powerful shift. You have to start making moves in your life to be better. Increase your stature, standards and status. Level Up! Level Up! Level Up! Be the authentic you. Your actions have to be pleasing to God. God took the heat so you can forget those things that are behind and press forward to those things of purpose within us.

Prayer

Lord, help me present my body and life daily for your glory.

Day 16
Journaling

Day 16

Authentic Expression

Day 17

Daily Devotional

<u>Make Room for Him</u>

Scripture

Matthew 6:21

KJV – For where your treasure is, there will your heart be also.

MSG – The place where your treasure is, is the place you will most want to be, and end up being.

AMP – For where your treasure is, there your heart {your wishes, your desires; that on wishes, your life centers} will be also.

Devotional Thought

We set our schedules. We know what we are doing on a daily basis. We set our calendar. We know when we need to be at work, a meeting, an event or activity. We spend hours daily on Facebook, Instagram, Twitter, YouTube and other internet platforms. We move about in our fast-paced society. We are consistently meeting deadlines for multiple projects. We clutter our day with so many different tasks. What has replaced your time with God? We make time for what we want. We have appointment cards to remind us of our next doctor's, hair, nail or spa appointment, but when was the last time you created space for God?

To honor God, we must declutter our lives. When we declutter our lives, it allows us to see Him. Find time to spend with Him. Identify today ways you can make room for Him. We have to make room for Him, God. God's everlasting presence makes all the difference. The intimate space allows us an opportunity to commune with Him. Diligently seek Him. His unconditional love is necessary. Time with God will align our desires with God's. Spending quality time with Him daily helps put everything else in perspective. What are ways we can make room for God? Ask God His plan for you. Read His Word, pray, journal your thoughts, meditate, study with a group or find an accountability partner. Whatever way God leads you, start today making room for Him. Write your plan today of how you will start spending time with God.

Prayer

Lord, show me today your plan for me to spend time with you.

Day 17
Journaling

Day 17
Authentic Expression

Day 18
Daily Devotional
<u>God's Timing Is Everything</u>

Scripture

Ecclesiastes 3:11

KJV – He hath made every thing beautiful in his time:

MSG – True, God made everything beautiful in itself and in its time---

AMP – He has made everything beautiful and appropriate in its time.

Devotional Thought

Timing is everything! Shout "God's time!" Ecclesiastes reminds us in verses 2-8 that there is "a time to be born and a time to die, a time to plant and a time to uproot, a time to kill and a time to heal, a time to tear down and a time to build, a time to weep and a time to laugh, a time to mourn and a time to dance, a time to scatter stones and a time to gather them, a time to embrace and a time to refrain from embracing, a time to search and a time to give up, a time to keep and a time to throw away, a time to tear and a time to mend, a time to be silent and a time to speak, a time to love and a time to hate, a time for war and a time for peace." Sometimes it seems like we won't get a break. It seems like God is not with us. When Lord? How long Lord? Why Lord? Where Lord? What Lord? These are the questions we start to ask. God's timing can feel like a long, extended, prolonged, lengthy, extensive and desperate delay. It seems like God is not going to intervene. I found that during these times, God is growing our faith, turning us towards Him. Spending more time with Him allows His Word to shape us, helping us wait and trust His timing. This is when God pulls us through. I have also found that it is here when it looks impossible that God gets involved. God shows up and manifests His promises. He gets the praises He deserves. We are in awe of Him and His presence. God gets all the GLORY! In the new testament, God's timing is referred to as "*Kairos,*" which means "appointed time in the purpose of God, the time when God acts." How will you respond in the wait? Write today the things you feel are taking a while to happen in your life. Ask God to show you what you need to do in this waiting season.

Prayer

Lord, help me wait on your timing so I can walk in your purpose.

Day 18
Journaling

Day 18

Authentic Expression

Day 19

Daily Devotional

<u>Hear Your Own Heartbeat</u>

Scripture

Ephesians 1:11

KJV – In whom also we have obtained an inheritance, being predestinated according to the purpose of him who worketh all things after the counsel of his own will.

MSG – It's in Christ that we find out who we are and what we are living for.

AMP – In Him also we have received an inheritance {a destiny—we were claimed by God as His own}, having been predestined (chosen, appointed beforehand) according to the purpose of Him who works everything in agreement with the counsel and design of His will.

Devotional Thought

What is it that brings you alive? What is it that you connect with? What is it that you feel rhythm with? What is that thing that brings you joy? What is the reason you get up in the morning? It could be your career, an interest, hobby or motivative aims. I call it my "heartbeat," the thing that I was created for and to do. Listen, hear your own heartbeat. What is flowing out of your heart? What is your heart saying to you? Know your purpose. What is purpose? *Purpose* is the plan or intent to do something. It is a desired result, goal and determination. Your purpose becomes the guiding light of your decisions, influence behaviors, directions which create meaning. In order to know who you are and your purpose, you have to ask God to show you so that you walk in your divine purpose. Your divine purpose is your intense passion, drive, design, duty, ambition and intent. Start today with a list of things you are passionate about. Awaken more to the reality for which God has created you. Start moving in the purpose-filled life God designed for you. Be the authentic you. Hear your own heartbeat. Do not get indulged with the noise of life. Continue to free yourself daily and be you. Live life the way God designed for YOU to live. Stay focused, look to God, show up and answer the call of purpose for your life. Set your face to please God only. This will keep you on His path. Push forward in your purpose. God will grace you in your forward movement. What are the things you desire to do? Write about your purpose today.

Prayer

Lord, open my ears, yes, and my heart so I can see, hear and know your purpose for my life.

Day 19
Journaling

Day 19

Authentic Expression

Day 20

Daily Devotional

<u>**Know Your WHY?**</u>

Scripture

Proverbs 19:21

KJV – There are many devices in a man's heart; nevertheless, the counsel of the Lord, that shall stand.

MSG – We humans keep brainstorming options and plans but God's purpose prevails.

AMP – Many plans are in a man's mind, But it is the Lord's purpose for him that will stand (be carried out).

Devotional Thought

It is your *why*. Your *why* pushes you to the best version of you. It is the reason you do the things you do. Your *why* comes from within. It is the thing that drives you to pursue what you really want to do, the God-given purpose. It is the thing that gives you meaning, the thing you enjoy and can't imagine yourself doing anything else. Ask yourself why do you do what you do? Ask yourself this question: Will this help you with identifying your sense of purpose, to find and do things that are meaningful to you? It can also help you identify what may be going wrong in your life so you can refocus, put things in perspective and move forward. Once you know your *why*, then your *what* has greater impact and you are able to move in your purpose. Brainstorm today. Ask yourself what you enjoy doing and why. What do you spend a lot of time doing? Everything about you has been for this moment. It is here you realized the things that happened to you had to happen for you to show up and answer the call of purpose. They produced your sound from your heartbeat. They all worked together for your good. Why? This is your reintroduction of you in a new and different way: delayed but not denied. You are here. You have arrived. These experiences have brought you to this place in integrity. This is your *why*.

Prayer

Thank you, Lord, for opening my eyes of understanding so I can know my *why*.

Day 20
Journaling

Day 20
Authentic Expression

Weekly Reflection &
Take Away

THE BIRTHING PLACE

The last four weeks you have had an opportunity to look at you. We started with the questions "who are you" and "who are you really?" We will refer to these moments as "the process." Everything you went through and all the labor pain moved you to this point. The process is always before the promise. You have had a chance to really look at you. The birthing place is where you can start writing your vision. You have been called, appointed and anointed to walk in your God-given purpose. When you walk in your purpose, you will not fit man's description. This is your time to focus on God, walk in God's timing, keep a servant's heart and write your vision.

During the next two weeks, you will seek God's directions for details and instructions to develop your vision and dream. It is time to step out. It is time to move forward! It is time to birth!
PUSH!!!!! PUSH!!!!! PUSH!!!!!

Day 21

Daily Devotional

<u>Lean on Him</u>

Scripture

Proverbs 3:5

KJV - Trust in the Lord with all thine heart; and lean not unto thine own understanding.

MSG - Trust God from the bottom of your heart; don't try to figure out everything on your own.

AMP - Trust in and rely confidently on the Lord with all your heart, And do not rely on your own insight or understanding.

Devotional Thought

The word *trust* means to depend on, have confidence, belief, reliance and assurance, to name a few, but what does it mean to you? Every day we move about with our trust in so many things. We trust our cars to take us where we want to go. We trust our jobs will be available. We trust after a week of work we will be paid. We trust people, family and friends. We trust our favorite team as sports fans. We trust celebrities. We trust politicians. We trust our immediate surroundings and we even trust ourselves. Why is it so easy for us to trust ourselves and so hard to trust God? This scripture reminds us to trust in Him with everything and for everything. He reminds us to not lean to us. Why? We do not have the ability to carry ourselves. We have to give him every part of us. He created us and He knows all about us. He has the ability to manage every area of our lives; He can handle us and everything that concerns us. Today give your gifts, talents, abilities, dream and vision to God. Write them down today and present them to Him. The return will be great!

Prayer

Lord, help me to trust You with everything concerning me. Amen!

Day 21

Journaling

Day 21

Authentic Expression

Day 22

Daily Devotional

Let Him Guide

Scripture

Proverbs 3:6

KJV - In all thy ways acknowledge him, and he shall direct thy paths.

MSG - Listen for God's voice in everything you do, everywhere you go; he's the one who will keep you on track.

AMP - In all your ways know and acknowledge and recognize Him, And He will make your path straight and smooth [removing obstacles that block your way].

Devotional Thought

So often we wake up in the morning preparing for the day without honoring the Father. We do not acknowledge Him. Start today. Take a moment before your feet hit the floor each morning to acknowledge Him. Acknowledge that He is the true and living God. Take a moment to admire Him. Take a moment to greet Him. Take a moment to recognize Him. Take a moment to praise Him. Take a moment to thank Him. Take a moment to welcome Him into this new day so that He can order your steps to make them straight and even, pleasant and prosperous. He is our guiding light. He deserves to be honored. We deserve His clear guidance and directions for our path.

Prayer

Lord, I acknowledge you. Give me directions today. I depend totally on you for guidance. Amen!

Day 22
Journaling

Day 22

Authentic Expression

Day 23

Daily Devotional

It's Working in You

Scripture

Ephesians 3:20

KJV - Now unto him that is able to do exceeding abundantly above all that we ask or think, according to the power that worketh in us.

MSG - God can do anything, you know-far more than you could ever imagine or guess or request in your wildest dream! He does it not by pushing us around but by working within us, his Spirit deeply and gently within us.

AMP – Now to Him who is able to [carry out His purpose and] do superabundantly more than all that we dare ask or think [infinitely beyond our greatest prayers, hopes or dreams], according to His power that is at work within us.

Devotional Thought

He goes beyond our thoughts. He goes beyond our expectations. He does more than average. He is qualified to do immeasurably more. He is extreme when it comes to you. God is able to multiply what you ask Him and what you think. What are the things that visit and speak to you daily? Is it a career, education, a personal or financial matter, or a family, business or spiritual goal? So often we allow our surroundings, lack and inadequate opportunities to speak to us, causing us to stop pursuing our passion. Your future, dreams and visions are worth fighting for. Confess your positive thoughts and visions daily. Declare the Word of God over your life daily. Open your mouth and speak to your future. Think on positive things. See yourself doing it. There is a power working in you. When God breathed in Adam, He breathed in you. There is a power working in you. The Greek word for power is *dunamis*, which means "ability and potential." The Spirit of God, the power of God is at work in your life. Tap into that place of your authentic, creative innovative self.

Prayer

Lord, help me tap into your Spirit that is at work in me daily. Amen!

Day 23

Journaling

Day 23
Authentic Expression

Day 24

Daily Devotional

<u>Now Walk It Out</u>

Scripture

James 2:26

KJV - For as the body without the spirit is dead, so faith without works is dead also.

MSG - The very moment you separate body and spirit, you end up with a corpse. Separate faith and works and you get the same thing: a corpse.

AMP - For as just as the [human] body without the spirit is dead, so faith without works [of obedience] is also dead.

Devotional Thought

You have to start movement towards your dreams and visions. You have to take actions toward your dreams and visions. You got to MOVE! Faith is when you do not see it, but you know it is possible. The Word of God reminds us that faith is the trust in God, the assurance of things, existence of things, hope for, divinely promised, vowed and the evidence, of our handle on the things we cannot see. I often think about a chair when I think about faith. Each day, we sit in some type of chair. We have the expectation, the hope that when we go to the chair, it will hold us up and provide for us a place to sit. What if the chair decided today it did not want to be a chair and it did not hold up to our expectations? So, it is with faith. It is expectation, trust, firm belief, confidence and reliance in God. We sit in the chair knowing it is going to come through for us and do just what we need it to do, hold us up. Things can be so much easier if we trust in God the same way. The same expectations we have for everyday life we have to have for our dreams and visions to keep them alive. When we are able to totally trust and believe God, we will see our dreams and visions come to pass.

Prayer

Lord, let me give myself to you. Strengthen my faith so I can walk in my destiny. Amen!

Day 24
Journaling

Day 24

Authentic Expression

Day 25

Daily Devotional

<u>*Just Do It*</u>

Scripture

Philippians 4:13

KJV - I can do all things through Christ which strengthened me.

MSG - Whatever I have, wherever I am, I can make it through anything in the One who makes me who I am.

AMP - I can do all things [which He has called me to do] through Him who strengthens and empowers me [to fulfill His purpose-I am self-sufficient in Christ's sufficiency; I am ready for anything and equal to anything through Him who infuses me with inner strength and confident peace.]

Devotional Thought

All means "the whole amount, quality on extent, as much as possible, the whole number or sum of" (Merriam Webster). *Strengthen* means "make or become stronger" (Oxford Languages).

God has equipped us to do all things! God is our strength; the one who strengthens us in every moment. God has graced us to fulfill our purpose and destiny! We can do whatever we want to do through Christ the Holy One, who has enabled us with strength, power and ability to complete the task. It is in Him we move, advance and make progress in our lives. Gird your loins and let Him be the wind of strength for you. You can do this! You are more than enough! God got YOU! Say to yourself, "I am able to do all things through Christ. I am strengthened to complete the course, path and purpose God has for my life." Continue to move forward.

Prayer

Thank you, Lord, for You are my strength. Amen!

Day 25
Journaling

Day 25

Authentic Expression

<u>Weekly Reflection &</u>
<u>Take Away</u>

Note to Self

Day 26

Daily Devotional

Write the Vision

Scripture

Habakkuk 2:2-3

KJV - And the Lord answered me, and said Write the vision, and make it plain upon tables, that he may run that readeth it.

MSG - And then God answered: Write this. Write what you see. Write it out in big block letters so that it can be read on the run.

AMP - Then the Lord answered me and said, "Write the vision and engrave it plainly out of [CLAY] tablets. So that the one who reads it will run for the vision is yet for the appointed [future] time.

Devotional Thought

Write means "to mark on a surface, typically paper, with a pen, pencil, or similar implement." *Oxford Languages*

What is meant by "write"? To put something in writing, to jot it down, to put it down, take a note, to take it down, to record it, to register it, to log it, to list it.

Write it down. What is the thing you often see? The thing you see so vividly every day, such as the thoughts you have visualized or envisioned. This is something you have seen yourself doing! The Word of God says "Write it down, put it in print and start today. Write down things that are important. It could be a picture, thought, plan or vision.

Write it down! Writing it down gives you ownership and holds you accountable for your visions. A vision requires an action plan. Writing your vision puts the plan in action. A vision without work is dead. Writing your vision is the beginning process of your faith for your vision. You are the first investor. My pen stands as a ready-writer, anticipating the next assignment.

Say to yourself, "Writing what I see helps my plans and thoughts come to be." Today, start writing you plans, visions and dreams down.

Prayer

Dear Lord, I thank you for entrusting me with vision. This day, I will become a ready writer, setting my future in motion. Amen!

Day 26
Journaling

Day 26
Authentic Expression

Day 27

Daily Devotional

<u>It Shall Come to Pass</u>

Scripture

Habakkuk 2:3

KJV - For the vision is yet for an appointed time, but at the end it shall speak, and not lie though it tarry, wait for it, because it will surely come, it will not tarry.

MSG - This vision-message is a witness pointing to what's coming. It aches for the coming- it can hardly wait! And it doesn't lie. If it seems slow in coming, wait. It is on its way. It will come right on time.

AMP - It hurries toward the goal [at fulfillment]; it will not fail. Even though it delays, wait [patiently] for it, because it will certainly come, it will not delay.

Devotional Thought

When I think about vision, I think about process. What is process? Process is going through different phases, steps, actions, challenges to achieve, reach, attain, accomplish an expected, set or particular end. In the process, there are times we will be disappointed, upset and maybe even feel like giving up because it seems as if what we have envisioned, longed for, planned, believed God for is just not going to happen. Oh no. But WAIT! The Word of God tells us to not get faint, weary or tired when we are doing well. Understand, hold fast, knowing that in due season, in a set time, we will accomplish the goal if we do not give up. Gird your loins, posture your shoulders, set your face because the visions, plans, dreams will come to pass. It may seem like it is taking a long time but during this time you are in the process. You are learning things about you. You are stopping old habits while you are learning a new skillset. You are learning what to do and what not to do so when the vision comes to pass, you are ready. Shout "I AM READY!" Let the devil know this means war and you have come to declare war on him and to get your stuff. This is not the time to give up; it is the time to go in. You have come too far; you have seen too much, and God is on your side. Rise up you warrior! Take your stand! Begin to see yourself doing it. Speak to it daily. Place it on your wall so you can see it daily. Run with the vision that it is coming to pass. God's promises are always "Yes and Amen." IT IS SO!

Today, start your vision board as a reminder of your vision.

Prayer

Dear Lord, give me clarity of the vision you have for my life. Amen!

Day 27
Journaling

Day 27

Authentic Expression

Day 28

Daily Devotional

Own the Room

Scripture

Jeremiah 17:7

KJV - Blessed is the man that trusteth in the Lord, and whose hope the Lord is.

MSG – But blessed is the man who trusts me, God.

AMP - Blessed [with spiritual security] is the man who believes and trust in and relies on the Lord And whose hope and confident expectation is the Lord.

Devotional Thought

On March 2020, I finished my last day of physical therapy at a facility in Greenville, South Carolina. I had been in therapy for several months. The receptionists at this facility were very friendly and we often had great conversation. I always enjoyed seeing them during my visits. On my last visit, I gave my goodbyes and told them I really enjoyed our conversations and meeting them. I left their office, headed to the elevator and I noticed someone behind me. It was one of the receptionists. I was thinking she must be headed out too, but to my surprise she was wanting my attention. She stopped me and said, "Ms. Deshields." I said, "Yes." She said, "How do you own the room?" With an ecstatic facial expression I responded, "Excuse me! I own the room?" She said, "Yes, how do you walk in and own the room?" I replied, "Wow! I didn't know I own the room. I just know I walk in God and I walk in confidence in Him. Therefore, with Him on my side, I have great confidence.

What this lady said that day stuck in my spirit for several days and I began to say, "I do own the room." I then began to ask God to show me how I own the room. This request wasn't to be arrogant, thinking I am better than others or disrespectful, but as Believers we do own the room. Owning the room means we are confident in God, we trust in Him, He is our guide, and we have great expectation that He will provide what we need. Owning the room means we have the audience's attention; we have the ability to influence others and we are aware of ourselves. When we are aware of ourselves and who we are in God, then we are not easily intimidated, fearful or afraid to walk in the room or sit at the table. We know in Him we are GREAT.

Find your greatness in Him! Own the room. Lift your head up and walk in your destiny. Go get everything God has promised you. I know you may have made some mistakes, felt left out, left alone, misunderstood or maybe felt you were not worth it, but square your shoulders and walk in the room. God is with you!!

Prayer

Dear God, drive out every fear with your mighty hand.
Help me stand tall in confidence in your presence. Amen!

Day 28

Journaling

Day 28

Authentic Expression

Day 29

Daily Devotional

Do YOU

Scripture

1 Corinthians 3:16, 17

KJV - Know ye not that ye are the temple of God, and that the Spirit of God dwelleth in you? If any man defiles the temple of God, him shall God destroy; for the temple of God is holy, which temple ye are.

MSG - You realize, don't you, that you are the temple of God, and God himself is present in you? No one will get by with vandalizing God's temple, you can be sure of that. God's temple is sacred—and you, remember, are the temple.

AMP - Do you not know and understand that you [the church] are the temple of God, and that the Spirit of God dwells [permanently] in you [collectively and individually]? If anyone destroys the temple of God [corrupting it with false doctrine], God will destroy the destroyer; for the temple of God is holy (sacred), and that is what you are.

Devotional Thought

Anxiety, fears and the state of uncertainty are at their peak. We are facing so many challenges that demand our time. Self-care is our opportunity to refine, boost, enhance or better ourselves. It is the moment to DO YOU! We are faced with challenges, which can cause us to lose ourselves in the movement of life.

One way we can take back control is to practice being aware. Be aware of the present moment. *Awareness* is being mindful of what is happening in the right now. This allows you to remove any disturbance of the past, anxieties for the future and provide a way to center yourself in the now. Try this exercise: Stop what you are doing, relax and go outside. Identify five thing you can see; four things you can hear; three things you can touch; two things you can smell; and one thing you can taste. This exercise will help you become aware of the present moment. It lifts your mood and reduces stress. Meditate. Take five minutes to sit quietly and follow your breath. This helps you feel more conscious and connected to the present. You can continue to do this frequently throughout the day to regroup as necessary.

Prayer

Dear Lord, I pray that my friends may enjoy good health and that all may go well with them, even as our souls are getting along well.

Day 29
Journaling

Day 29
Authentic Expression

Day 30

Daily Devotional

Live Your Story

Scripture

Proverbs 16:9

KJV - A man's heart deviseth his way: but the Lord directeth his steps.

MSG – We plan the way we want to live, but only God makes us able to live it.

AMP – A man's mind plans his way [as he journeys through life], But the Lord directs his steps and establishes them.

Devotional Thought

What's really important to you? As you start living your story, you will find people and opportunities being drawn to you. Everything you went through is for now. Don't push yourself on the stage; prepare yourself for it. When you walk in your purpose, you walk differently. Even when challenges arise, you have the confidence of knowing you can face them because it is part of the process and the plan of God. This is your story in the making, fully expressed by you. Live the life God planned for you to live. Follow the passions, dreams and visions God has designed for your life. It's time to live a life of joy, fulfillment and passion by moving and taking action in the direction of your dreams. When living your story, you have to have a balance with your spiritual, social, emotional, physical and financial. Have a balance between your career, relationship, creative expression and personal development. Make sure you are aware and stay connected to the authentic you. Stage your life. Journey through each moment and live your story. Let the Light of God come shining through. You are a shining star, shining brightly in your path and lighting the way for others. Tell and sell your story. So many people are waiting on you to give out what God has given to you. Share your story with the world. God shared His Glory so you can share your story.

Prayer

Dear God, order my steps! Amen!

Day 30
Journaling

Day 30
Authentic Expression

<u>*Weekly Reflection &*</u>

<u>*Take Away*</u>

Note to Self

_____

_____

_____

_____

_____

_____

_____

_____

_____

_____

_____

_____

_____

_____

_____

Note to Self

Acknowledgements

I would like to thank my family, my Godmothers Sally Boseman and Willie Fant, my Godchildren, my wonderful friends Paula Bruce, Alexis Payton, LaTasla Gardner, Pamela Byrd-Nipper, Lucila Beaton, Lisa Anderson, my artist Patro Ulmer, The Zone Partners, Love Zone Ministry, The Zone Dream Team, Dr. Sonia Cunningham Leverette and Hadassah's Crown Publishing for your love, prayers and support.

About the Author

Treca Yvette DeShields is the Founder of *The Zone,* a multicultural community service center whose mission is to provide services that build trusting relationships with youth and families.

Born and reared in Clinton, South Carolina to Mary DeShields and Thomas Glenn, Treca has dedicated many hours and a lot of energy to the small town. She graduated from Clinton High School in 1989 and obtained a Bachelor of Science Degree in Child and Family Development from Benedict College in 1994. She completed her Master's Degree in Social Work from the University of South Carolina in 2011. Throughout her tenure, Treca has served her community by working to ensure access, resources and opportunities for youth and families.

In March 1990, Treca's life was transformed in more ways than one. She suffered a brutal assault during which she was stabbed nine times, a hair's breadth from death when one of the wounds almost severed a main artery in her neck. Prior to the incident that left her physically and emotionally scarred, Treca was at a spiritual crossroads in her life. She contemplated completely surrendering to God, but she was unable to make a full commitment. A near-death experience on the operating table after she was stabbed left her with an ultimatum from God. She could remain in the afterlife, or she could return and spend her renewed life serving God. She chose the latter.

Treca's newfound purpose and lifelong youth ambassadorship led to her first venture: Save Our Youth (S.O.Y.) Choir in Clinton, South Carolina. Established in 1990, it served as a positive platform for the children of the community to express themselves through spiritual songs and praise, as well as learn to relate to one another as members of the body of Christ. The 100-voice choir has traveled throughout the United States, opening for gospel choirs and performing gospel plays written by Treca herself. Save Our Youth Choir was only the beginning of a simple vision that later developed into a multi-faceted youth, family and community outreach organization, Future Leader Center of America.

As Treca continued working with youth in the Clinton area, she saw the need for quality, affordable childcare. New Generation Early Learning Center (currently Future Leader Center for Development) was established in May 1994. With a mission to prepare leaders to lead the nation, the center grew in popularity. In March 2004, another center was opened in Anderson, and the Clinton center was downsized to group home day care.

Continuing on her journey of supporting youth, Treca founded The Zone in 2011. The Zone partners with various entities in the community to provide more effective services and build natural support systems. Some programs and events the organization provide include: Target 111, an emergency food bank in Laurens County; Creating Opportunities Reaching Everyone (C.O.R.E.), an outreach program that focuses on life skills, math, reading, and workforce development; First Saturday Exchange, an event through the C.O.R.E. program that allows community members to purchase items from upcoming entrepreneurs and artists at low costs; and much more.

In addition to her work with youth, Treca is also a member of Delta Sigma Theta Sorority, Inc., a minister, songstress, motivational speaker, business consultant, certified grant writer, and therapeutic support specialist. She is the founder of Kazan Event & Catering, Expression of Love and Love Zone Ministry. Treca has served on several boards and fulfilled other roles with various organizations throughout the Upstate of South Carolina.

Author Contact Information

treca.deshields71@gmail.com
864-933-6343
Facebook Treca DeShields

HadassahsCrownPublishing.com

HadassahsCrown@gmail.com

864-708-1214